Original title:
Grassblade Gospels

Copyright © 2025 Creative Arts Management OÜ
All rights reserved.

Author: Fiona Harrington
ISBN HARDBACK: 978-1-80566-719-3
ISBN PAPERBACK: 978-1-80566-848-0

## Whispers of the Verdant Choir

In fields where daisies dance and sway,
The grass sings secrets in its play.
It tickles toes and begs for cheer,
While ants hold meetings far and near.

A wise old blade with stripes of green,
Claims it's the wisest ever seen.
With jokes about the windy days,
It cracks us up in sunlit rays.

## Hymn of the Silent Meadow

The meadow hums a tune so grand,
With bunnies playing in the sand.
They leap and jump, a comical sight,
While butterflies dance, oh what a flight!

A snail's a slowpoke, but has the flair,
It takes its time without a care.
Singing softly to the grass,
"Let's take our time, life's here to pass!"

## From Roots to Canopy

The roots are gossiping down below,
While trunks are swaying in the flow.
A squirrel tells tales of daring feats,
While leaves just laugh, sharing their treats.

"Why'd the acorn cross the road?"
To find a tree, oh what a load!
With giggles echoing through the air,
Nature's humor is everywhere!

**Secrets Beneath the Green**

Beneath the blades a drama brews,
With worms that throw a party ruse.
They wiggle and twist, dressed up in style,
While crickets chirp and sway awhile.

A laughing fern whispers to the shade,
Of grasshoppers' pranks and masquerade.
"Join us here, let's celebrate!"
Under the sky, we'll liberate!

## Parables of the Flourishing Earth

In a garden of giggles, tulips dance,
The daisies gossip, oh what a chance.
Bumblebees buzz with a ticklish cheer,
While earthworms squirm, spreading joy far and near.

Sunflowers wear glasses, looking so bright,
They squint at the clouds, oh what a sight!
A rabbit hops by in a polka-dot vest,
The joy of the soil, a wild, happy quest.

The carrots are chatting, plotting a game,
While ladybugs boast of their world-famous fame.
A snail tells a tale, slow in his ways,
Of running marathons in sunny, lazy days.

The onions are crying, but don't shed a tear,
They're just laughing too hard, oh what a dear.
In this quirky plot of sunshine and mirth,
Nature's own whimsy, a comical birth.

## Verses from the Meadow's Heart

The meadow is laughing, bursting with glee,
As squirrels put on shows, oh can't you see?
A butterfly twirls, trying to lead,
While ants in a line plot their next big seed.

With daisies as speakers, they boast with pride,
About the best picnic spots to abide.
A bumblebee hiccups from sipping too sweet,
Spills nectar on flowers, oh what a feat!

The grass tickles toes, what a delight,
A frog in a tuxedo hops with a bite.
He croaks a fine joke, the snails start to snicker,
As the sun starts to blush, the day gets much quicker.

The wind sings a tune, making all sway,
The meadow's a stage, come dance, come play!
In this vibrant bouquet, humor takes flight,
Life's simple pleasures shine ever so bright.

## Fables of the Rolling Fields

In rolling green hills where mischief is sown,
The sheep tell tall tales, oh how they've grown.
With woolly jackets, they strut and they prance,
Never a worry, always up for a chance.

The cows play the drums, mooing a beat,
While chasing the clouds on their light, happy feet.
A fox in a top hat gives speeches galore,
About how to get snacks from the local farm store.

The flowers all giggle, a colorful crew,
Sharing wild stories about the morning dew.
A gopher with glasses, reading his book,
Injects all the fun with each teasing look.

One chicken throws parties with eggs on a plate,
Dancing all night, oh isn't it great?
The fields hum a tune, full of jest and jest,
In this land of laughter, life's a joyous fest.

## The Leaf's Silent Testament

In whispers of breezes, the leaves start to talk,
They share silly secrets while twirling a walk.
A pumpkin near giggles, covered in vines,
Clutches a parrot that spouts rhyming lines.

Roots play charades beneath earthy cheer,
While mushrooms do ballet, bringing giggles near.
A squirrel sets a record for fastest nut chase,
With a crowd of peas watching, they clap and embrace.

The sun gets a chuckle from clouds in the sky,
Who've dressed up as creatures, oh my, oh my!
Top hats and bowties on various shades,
Nature's own circus, where joy never fades.

So here's to the laughter, so pure and so wise,
In a leafy communion beneath sunny skies.
Each fluttering sound, a joyful decree,
In this gentle haven, life thrives wild and free.

## The Tune of the Thicket's Embrace

In a thicket where we giggle,
The squirrels dance with a wiggle.
A rabbit slips in a patch of clover,
Wonders if he'll ever find a four-leafed lover.

The hedgehog sings in a very sharp tone,
While frogs croak loud, but sing alone.
A tangle of vines makes a funny hat,
And the wise old owl just laughs at that.

## Whispers from the Verdant Tapestry

The grass whispers tales to the wandering breeze,
Of chubby ants marching with utmost ease.
A ladybug joins in, dressed oh so bright,
As the flowers laugh at them, what a silly sight!

The dandelions puff like grand balloons,
As bees trip over their own funny tunes.
With every sway of this leafy place,
Nature cracks jokes with a leafy grace.

## Meditations in the Meadow's Embrace

In the meadow where daisies dream,
A frog contemplates his next big scheme.
He's planned to leap to the moon by night,
But ends up tripping on worms in flight.

Butterflies giggle and scatter about,
Wondering seriously what the fuss is about.
They take turns swirling while sipping sweet dew,
Joking with blades of grass, making a queue.

## Ballet of the Blooming Grass

In a field where the blooms twirl and sway,
A dandelion pirouettes, come what may.
The flowers all giggle at this brave show,
As the bees buzz rounds like they're part of the flow.

A curious rabbit tries a grand leap,
But lands in a patch where the flowers do weep.
They tickle him back, and he rolls with delight,
In laughter and tumble, they dance through the night.

## Aria of the Quiet Growth

In the yard where daisies sprout,
A snail slides by, no fear, no doubt.
With a shell so bright, it's quite a sight,
He dreams of speed, but stays out of sight.

The ants parade, a tiny line,
With crumbs in tow, they march just fine.
Yet every now and then they frown,
For one lost ant, he's turned around.

## Legends of the Swaying Hay

Wiggly worms beneath the grass,
They gossip loudly, none can pass.
The blades around them twist and twirl,
As their silly secrets start to swirl.

The fluttering leaves hold a dance,
As the breeze gives each a chance.
And if you listen, laughter grows,
From ticklish roots and silly toes.

## Fables of the Gentle Undergrowth

A squirrel leaps with little grace,
Chasing shadows in a hasty pace.
He trips on twigs, falls with a thud,
And blames it all on the grass and mud.

In the thickets, frogs wear crowns,
Croaking tunes that often drown.
They hold a concert, such a show,
But all the flies just steal the glow.

## The Muffled Cries of Nature

The beetles boast of strength and might,
But struggle just to take off flight.
Their shiny shells reflect the sun,
But land on backs—oh, what a fun!

A dandelion frees its seeds,
A gust of wind fulfills their needs.
They float about, a wild parade,
While wishes linger, dreams are made.

## Archives of the Blooming Silence

In the garden where whispers dwell,
Flowers gossip, can you tell?
Petals giggle with a flair,
Telling secrets without a care.

Bees buzz by with a zany tune,
While daisies dance beneath the moon.
Old toad sings, a croaky jest,
Claiming the frogs are simply the best.

A snail slips by with style so sleek,
Claiming victory, so bold, so chic.
Each blade of grass knows just the joke,
To tickle the weeds and make them choke.

When breezes laugh and tickle the buds,
Nature's pranks flow like tiny floods.
In silence, blooms speak a truth so bright,
With laughter hidden, just out of sight.

## The Treasures of Overgrown Pathways

On pathways where wildflowers grow,
Each step reveals a hidden show.
Mossy rocks wear a cheeky grin,
While beetles race, let the fun begin!

Vines twist tales of old and new,
Raccoons join in, sing a tune or two.
Crickets form a band, don't you see?
Making music with glee and harmony.

A frog recites poetry, so absurd,
Joking 'bout flies, oh what a nerd!
Lizards cheer and clap so loud,
While sunbeams filter through the crowd.

In overgrown corners, laughter blooms,
As flowers plot out their funny dooms.
Each pathway hides treasures of mirth,
In this wacky, wild rebirth.

## Melodies of the Wildflower Muse

In fields where wildflowers break the mold,
The sun's warmth sings, a tale retold.
A poppy shimmies, a breeze so sweet,
Twirling with joy on the grass beneath.

Bumblebees stage a buzzing show,
With tiny hats that steal the glow.
Forget-me-nots giggle, sharing the scene,
As butterflies flaunt their wings of green.

Dandelions puff with a most silly pose,
Claiming they spread wisdom wherever they go.
While clovers wink with four-leaved charms,
Drawing in luck with their leafy arms.

Each petal notes a melody bright,
A chorus of colors in dappled light.
With nature's humor at the core,
Laughter lingers forevermore.

## Beneath the Heaven's Canopy

Under the sky where clouds play tricks,
Raindrops laugh, you'll hear the kicks.
Squirrels spin tales of acorn fame,
While earthworms giggle at their simple game.

Tall trees gossip, branches swaying,
Like old friends in a lighthearted playing.
Each breeze carries whispers so warm,
Telling tales of nature's charm.

Sunlight hides, peeking through leaves,
As nature's jokes weave through the eaves.
A chipmunk rolls, a comic runaway,
Stumbling 'round, it brightens the day.

Beneath the canopy, mirth takes flight,
As laughter dances through day and night.
In the wild, every giggle is true,
With nature's heart, ever so askew.

## The Awakening of Green Spirits

In the early bud's chatter, they plot,
Mossy hats on their heads, not a single thought.
With giggles of dew, they tease through the day,
While worms tell their tales in a wiggle-fish way.

A dandelion danced, oh what a sight,
Swaying to tunes sung by bees taking flight.
They laugh at the clouds, so fluffy and white,
Chasing their shadows, from morning to night.

## Serene Stories from the Swarth

Beneath a wide oak, the critters convene,
Sharing tall tales that are silly and keen.
A squirrel makes claims that are far from the truth,
Claiming a nut is worth more than a tooth.

The clovers all whisper, oh what a name,
For grasshoppers hopping in a grasshopper game.
They contest with each other, with laughter and glee,
One leaps for the moon, while the others just flee.

**Prose from the Verdant Silence**

The sun barely peeks, but stories abound,
With petals and leaves shaking their sound.
A snail writes a novel, slow but sincere,
While ants publish gossip that's loudly unclear.

"Did you hear about Fern?" says a blade with a grin,
"She thought she was Buddha, but lost in the wind!"
They chuckle in whispers, from stalk to sweet root,
While ladybugs gossip in each striped suit.

## The Voice Beneath the Underbrush

Where shadows entwine, and mischief does lurk,
A tale-telling beetle has found quite a perk.
With a monocle perched, he shares with great pride,
Of snickers and giggles that worms cannot hide.

Optical weeds stretch, jostling for space,
In a comedy show, they find their own grace.
With snorts and with snickers — oh what a mess!
Each laughding ignites, all chaos, no stress!

## The Lush Lament

In a field where laughter hides,
The dandelions have their pride.
They wiggle and dance in the sun,
Challenging hawks just for fun.

The daisies gossip, "Hey, look here!"
"Why do those weeds look so queer?"
A patch of clover shouts, "Join in!"
While ants parade with cheeky grins.

The tall grass sways and bends its back,
"A soft breeze brings a playful smack."
But snails just dream of speed and flair,
While worms roll doubles in midair!

So let us toast with blades of green,
To fields of laughter, pure and keen!
With roots that tickle all around,
In nature's fun, true joy is found.

## Prism of the Meadow's Soul

A meadow bright with colors grand,
Where butterflies play and daisies stand.
The sunbeams giggle on the leaves,
Tickling petals like playful thieves.

The crickets launch a nighttime show,
With chirps that bounce and ebb just so.
They strut their stuff on silken threads,
While fireflies dance above our heads.

In this patch where oddballs thrive,
A worm in glasses claims to drive!
The bees compete in buzzing speed,
Their honey jokes plant quite the seed.

Let's celebrate the zany glow,
Of nature's quirks that steal the show!
In every leaf, a laugh is spun,
While grasshoppers leap, just for fun!

## **Truths in the Gentle Breeze**

The breeze whispers secrets, all aglow,
Tickling my ears, making me know.
That ladybugs plot a grand parade,
With antlers made from sweet charade.

A squirrel nearby cracks acorn wit,
As branches giggle, not giving a hit.
The blooms all nod in vibrant cheer,
While frogs chant songs we can't quite hear.

The clouds above gossip, wide and free,
Daring raindrops to join their spree.
"I can splatter, just you wait!"
Says one bold drop, "Before it's late!"

So let the winds spin tales of mirth,
As all creatures join in for the birth.
Of joy in each rustle and sigh,
In nature's giggle, we all fly high.

## Elegy of the Wandering Blade

A lone blade wanders, far and wide,
With dreams of soaring, feeling pride.
"Why's everyone so rooted here?
Join me on this quest, have no fear!"

The daisies chuckle, "Oh, dear mate!
Your dreams are grand, but can you skate?"
While violets tease with winks of mirth,
"Come back to earth, you know your worth!"

But off it sways, in daring flight,
Chasing sunbeams with all its might.
It bumps in clouds, feels skies above,
Finding freedom in the push and shove.

Yet somewhere deep, it knows the truth,
That even blades need roots for proof.
So soon it twirls, then heads back home,
With laughter echoing where it roamed.

## Green Harmony of the Earthbound.

In a field where cows think they can fly,
A sheep in shades of pink caught my eye.
They promised a feast of grass so divine,
But only found salad dressed in decline.

The daisies giggle as the sun gets bright,
A broccoli tree claims it's quite the sight.
With every breeze, the flowers sway,
While bees parade in a jolly ballet.

Crickets play tunes on a leafy stage,
While ladybugs dance like they're on a rampage.
The worms hold a meeting under the clover,
Claiming they're tired of being pushovers.

So let's raise a toast, dear friends of the green,
To laughter and joy in a world so serene.
With a grasshopper DJ, we'll never be bored,
In this funny world, we'll never be floored.

## **Whispers of the Meadow**

In the meadow where whispers play,
A squirrel holds court, ruling the hay.
With acorns in hand, he plots and schemes,
For the grandest harvest of autumn dreams.

Butterflies flutter, gossiping loud,
Sharing secrets to an amused crowd.
The daisies blush at a joke from a bee,
While grasshoppers chuckle, sipping their tea.

A frog croaks jokes on his lilypad throne,
All the critters laugh till they moan.
With a hop and a leap, they dance around,
In this meadow of mirth, joy knows no bound.

So gather, dear friends, in laughter we meet,
For nature's own jesters, make life oh-so sweet.
In whispers and giggles, the day drifts away,
As the sun sets softly, painting skies of gray.

## Songs of the Verdant Whisper

The grass sings softly underfoot,
With a rhythm that's charming and quite astute.
A hedgehog hums in a dubious tune,
Dreaming of mushrooms beneath the moon.

Leaves sway gently, a dance in the breeze,
While squirrels debate the best kind of cheese.
"Oh cheddar!" cries one, "It's clearly the best,
But gouda can't be beaten at a fun fest!"

A rabbit in shades struts with delight,
Claiming he's now the king of the night.
While the fireflies twinkle, tossing their light,
Chasing off worries, making wrongs right.

So join in the chorus, sing with all glee,
For nature's own ballads set our spirits free.
With a giggle and wiggle, we'll dance till we fall,
In this verdant abode, fun is for all.

## Echoes Beneath the Canopy

Beneath the trees where the critters convene,
A raccoon reveals it's not quite a machine.
With shiny objects, he's quite the collect,
And nothing can stop his crafty intellect.

A snail holds council on the mossy path,
Declaring a war against the morning's wrath.
"I declare," he shouts with a slimy flair,
"Tomorrow, we'll march, but first, nap and share!"

The owls exchange tales of their late-night snacks,
While lizards practice their stand-up acts.
With each hoot and chirp, laughter unfolds,
As nature's humor simply never grows old.

So take a seat on the tallest of logs,
And join the antics of frogs and their fogs.
With echoes of joy in the boughs overhead,
We'll relish the laughter that nature has bred.

## The Silent Dialogue of the Field

In the field, whispers float,
Grains gossip and goats take note.
The daisies nod, all in jest,
While the sunflowers claim they're the best.

Worms hold court beneath the dirt,
Fashion discussions on how to flirt.
"Do you think the rain will tease?"
"Only if the wind's not a breeze!"

Ants debate who's the fastest sprinter,
While ladybugs share a quiet splinter.
They all giggle at the clouds above,
And tease the robins about their love.

The field, a stage of nature's lore,
Where every blade has tales galore.
With a wink and a chuckle so sly,
The grass sings, and the daisies sigh.

## Incantations from the Verdant Sanctuary

In the garden, secrets brew,
With herbs plotting what they'll do.
Mint flirts with thyme over tea,
While basil claims, "It's all about me!"

Petunias gather for chants at night,
While crickets play a chorus of fright.
"Do we sing to the moon or the sun?"
"Let's aim for both; that sounds like fun!"

Roses prance with a thorny twist,
Daring the bees to dance or resist.
"Is that perfume? No, it's just me!"
"Next time, bring honey, do decree!"

The verdant sanctuary laughs in delight,
As squirrels throw acorns with all their might.
Their magic swirls with a playful grace,
Nature's rascals in this sacred space.

## **Reflections in Green Waters**

In ponds where the frogs hold court,
They croak out tales of their last sport.
"Did you leap further than your mate?"
"Only when the dragonfly was late!"

Lilies lounge, striking goofy poses,
While fish joke about their scaly noses.
"Is it hot in here, or just me?"
"Nope, just the sun, can't you see?"

The reeds sway with whispers of sass,
Sharing secrets from green blades of grass.
"Maybe we should have a dance tonight!"
"Only if we don't scare away the light!"

In reflections where laughter flows,
The green waters teach us how joy grows.
With splashes of humor and tales galore,
Nature's jesters leave us wanting more.

## Harmonies of the Flourishing Horizons

On the hills where daisies sway,
The wind delivers wild ballet.
Clouds join in, a fluffy troupe,
While bunnies hop and start to droop.

Butterflies take center stage,
Twisting and twirling, a bright page.
"Can you keep up with my flair?"
"Only if you don't fly in the air!"

The sun winks down on the vibrant scene,
Proud of the colors—gold and green.
"Let's have a picnic, grab a seat!"
"Only if the ants don't want to eat!"

Horizons laugh with each passing breeze,
Tickling the flowers, swaying the trees.
In a world where each moment's a song,
Nature's harmony keeps us lifelong.

## Reflections in the Dewdrop Mirror

A dewdrop glimmers bright,
Reflecting clouds in flight.
A little ant walks by,
In his tiny, dapper tie.

The droplet holds a grin,
As grass blades jest and spin.
"Who's the fairest of us here?"
The gopher giggles near.

Each droplet tells a tale,
Of bugs and wind without fail.
They dance beneath the sun,
Laughing—oh, what fun!

In the mirror's gentle sway,
Nature's jokes come out to play.
So next time you look close,
You'll hear the giggles, almost.

## Lessons from the Wandering Breeze

A breeze blew through the field,
With secrets yet concealed.
"Hey there, cow, why so glum?"
"Lost my way and barely come!"

The trees chuckled loud and clear,
"Just follow your own cheer!"
The breeze tangled her hair,
"No need to fret, just breathe the air."

A butterfly flapped by,
With a wink and a sly sigh.
"Chase your dreams, don't delay!"
And off she fluttered away.

So if you feel like a mess,
Just dance—it's anyone's guess!
The breeze can't steer you wrong,
Embrace where you belong!

## **Scribe of the Rustling Reeds**

In a marsh where the reeds sigh,
A scribe writes with a glance sky-high.
"Mosquitoes make the best ink,"
He quips while taking a drink.

He pens the tales of frogs at night,
Who croak and leap in moonlight.
"Dear reader, hold your breath,
The bullfrog's got a laugh that's death!"

The wind whispers, "What a show!
Join the fun, come on, let's go!"
The reeds begin to sway along,
Creating nature's funny song.

So if you stroll by the bog,
Listen close, you'll hear the dialogue.
For the scribe knows, with wit so keen,
Life's humor in all that's green!

## The Eternal Dance of Roots and Sky

Beneath the earth, the roots convene,
In a dance so wild and serene.
"Up above, it's a party, too,
So let's swing and boogie in the dew!"

The clouds shake hands with the grass,
As squirrels race each other fast.
"Who knew the sky had rhythm?"
A wise old owl begins the hymn.

The flowers twirl in colorful threads,
As worms groove on their heads.
"Don't forget to do the twist!"
The daisies cheer—none can resist!

In this joint so lively and light,
Roots and sky dance till the night.
So grab a leaf and jump around,
Join the whimsy underground!

# Light Dances on the Grass

The sun peeked out, a golden laugh,
While ants held court upon their path.
A butterfly flitted, dressed in bright,
Winking at daisies, oh what a sight!

A squirrel tried to dance, lost in the beat,
Tripped on a twig, oh, what a feat!
The shadows chuckled, they swayed along,
Joining in nature's silly song.

With every breeze, the grasses swirled,
Tickling toes as the fun unfurled.
A ladybug joined as the jester in green,
Making the day a joyful routine.

So come join the laughter, let's frolic and play,
Where the light dances 'til the end of the day.
The world is a stage, the grass is the floor,
In this green land, who could ask for more?

## Nature's Benevolent Proclamation

A whispering breeze shared secret news,
While toads declared, 'Choose your favorite shoes!'
Daisies giggled, under clouds so wide,
"Wear mismatched socks, wear 'em with pride!"

A crow raised a toast with a shiny lost key,
"Here's to the worms… they serve fancy tea!"
The frogs croaked a tune, a merry old sound,
Celebrating joys that naturally abound.

A hedgehog captain perched on a log,
While ants held a meeting, tossing ideas like fog.
"Let's plant confetti and dance in the rain!"
Nature's accord, a playful campaign.

With laughter echoing, day after day,
The flora conspired in a whimsical way.
Proclaim to the world, the land and the air,
Join in the laughter, there's plenty to share!

## **The Green Path Manifesto**

The path made of grass, we swear to obey,
With daisies as leaders, come join the fray.
We pledge to twirl, to skip and to roll,
And promise to honor each silly soul.

Grassy green meetings, where giggles arise,
We'll trade all our secrets for cookie supplies.
The hedges nod, in their leafy attire,
While crickets compose tunes to inspire.

Let's paint the world with our laughter and cheer,
Bring out all the fruit, let's have a grand beer!
The sun is our witness, the earth is our stage,
In this merry gathering, we flip the last page.

With each little joke that bounces around,
The green path's agenda is joyfully found.
So gather your friends, don't be in a rush,
The manifesto is clear: it's time for a plush!

## Testament of the Leafy Scribe

There once was a leaf with tales to share,
A scribe of the grass, with secrets to spare.
"Once I saw raindrops do a tango divine,
And a worm who recited a nursery rhyme!"

In the shade of a bough, the stories flew free,
Of bumblebee bard's sweet symphony spree.
A caterpillar rapped, so rhythmically proud,
"I'll be a butterfly soon! Watch out for my crowd!"

Frogs croaked applause with their pondside cheer,
As leaves turned the pages, with joy and good cheer.
"Let's write of the days filled with laughter and light,
And the mischief we cause under stars that shine bright."

So if you find shade beneath branches so wide,
Just listen intently, take joy in the ride.
For the scribe of the leaf holds adventures galore,
In the heart of the green, always wanting more!

## The Language of Forgotten Leaves

In the breeze, leaves start to chat,
They're giggling under a big old hat.
A squirrel scolds, 'Don't you dare fall!'
The laughter ripples through them all.

Once proud, they dance, now dust on the ground,
Sharing secrets, oh, the tales abound!
What's red when ripe, then brown when it's not?
The story of leaves is tricky, I thought!

They whisper tales of a long-lost cheer,
Of picnics past and that dog named Pierre.
Throwing leaves like confetti in spring,
Who knew they could be such delightful thing?

So next time you stroll through the vibrant wood,
Listen closely, they'll share what they could.
For in each rustle, there's giggles and glee,
A playful language for you and for me.

## Chronicles of the Whispering Field

Fields of green, with tales to tell,
Where daisies gossip, and clovers dwell.
A rabbit hops, saying, 'What's the news?'
The corn sways back, 'Just your usual snooze!'

They chat about weather, a storm brewing near,
And how the farmer will come with his gear.
A sunflower boasts of its height to the sky,
While the humble grass chuckles, 'Give me a try!'

In between giggles, the crickets dance,
As the flowers twirl in a whimsical trance.
"Who ordered the rain?" The wildflowers croon,
"Let's hope it's not just another monsoon!"

So when you cross the fields, take a pause,
Hear their laughter, and give them applause.
For in this patchwork of life so surreal,
The chronicles spin in the whispering field.

**Verses in the Wind**

The wind carries whispers through trees so old,
Of mischief and pranks that have never grown cold.
"Did you see that crow steal my shiny key?"
The poppies exclaim, "Oh, you're so funny!"

With every gust, a new story flows,
Of daring adventures and ticklish toes.
The breeze tickles leaves; they giggle and quake,
What folly is here? What fun will we make?

Dandelions puff while singing their tune,
'We're the stars tonight, watch us glow like the moon!'
A mischievous wind responds with a sigh,
'You'll be made of fluff soon, oh my, oh my!'

So let the wind carry your laughter and song,
For verses in wind are where we belong.
In the dance of the trees, the fun never ends,
As nature unveils her wittiest rends.

## Green Stanzas of the Soul

In the garden, where green fingers tease,
Chasing shadows, dancing with bees.
"Why do you buzz?" asks a stubborn old fern,
'And why do you spin? Look at how I turn!'

The daisies debate over who's really the best,
While the thistles just laugh, taking a rest.
"A thorn's just a defense," the roses insist,
But the violets giggle, "Oh, you's on the list!"

With every petal and every sprout,
The garden sings songs that turn inside out.
For in every color, a stanza does play,
Telling tales of the fun they see every day.

So when you wander through nature's embrace,
Listen for laughter, and join in the race.
For in these green stanzas of whimsical glee,
The heart of the world is forever set free.

**The Canvas of Climbers and Crawlers**

A worm in a turtleneck, quite the sight,
Fashion trends underground, oh what a fright!
Beetles hold fashion shows on their way,
While ants take a selfie, posing in gay.

A snail glides by, with his shell so chic,
He's the runway star, every week, so unique.
Mice wear tiny hats, with a feather on top,
In this patch of green, the laughter won't stop.

In the shade of the grass, the critters meet,
With gossip and giggles, their lives so sweet.
Frogs plan a flash mob, croaking with flair,
While the fireflies dance, lighting up the air.

In the kaleidoscope world beneath our feet,
Each character prances, none know defeat!
So if you're feeling blue, just stoop down low,
And join the parade where the fun seeds grow.

## **Chants from the Blades Below**

Under the green, a choir does sing,
With ants in tuxedos, it's quite a thing.
Grasshoppers hop, keeping rhythm just right,
While worms play the harp, twinkling through night.

Crickets are crooning, their love songs so bold,
To the glow of the moon, stories unfold.
Even the raindrops join in the tune,
As the earth hums along to the jolly monsoon.

Hedgies in tuxes are dancing with glee,
The moss is a ballpark, come join the spree!
From roots up to blades, there's giggles galore,
In this underground jam, who could want more?

As music floats higher, do give it a try,
With laughter and cheer, to the stars we will fly.
For each note that rings in this sprawling expanse,
Is a tune soaked in mirth, urging all to dance.

## The Testament of the Whistling Wind

A breeze sneaked in, with a tickle and swish,
Said secrets of squirrels are all his wish.
He carries their whispers from tree to tree,
Making grass giggle, like it's thirsty for tea.

The dandelions sway, with a chuckle and pop,
As cows hear the gossip and give a soft 'Moo' drop.
The wind tells tall tales of the clouds up above,
And swirls round the flowers, spreading the love.

'You couldn't catch me,' the zephyr croons raw,
With each gust, it teases, leaving us in awe.
Even the daisies lean in to hear,
With petals a-flutter, thrilled with bright cheer.

So if ever it whistles, just halt and just pause,
For humor's a gem, found in nature's own cause.
The wind's got a story, hilariously spun,
If you listen closely, you'll catch the fun!

## **Verses from the Earth's Expanse**

Under the surface lies the world of the jest,
With playful roly-polies, who never get stressed.
They roll down the hills, in a giggly spree,
While the earthworms debate who's the best at their spree.

The flowers hold court, blooming in array,
They share aromatic jokes every sunny day.
With petals like fans, they laugh and they tease,
Creating a scene that's meant to appease.

In the shade of the leaves, the shadows do shimmy,
As snails tell tall tales, their stories so skimmy.
An acorn gets pranked by the nuts on the vine,
While the hedgehogs chuckle and sip on sweet wine.

So roam through the grass, in this jovial realm,
Where laughter is currency, we all take the helm.
For beneath every petal, and behind every stone,
Lives a world filled with comedy, never alone.

## Hymns of Nature's Expanse

In fields where daisies wear their crowns,
The ants have started silly towns.
They dance in pairs on tiny feet,
While grasshoppers play the lively beat.

A rabbit sings with squeaky voice,
And cabbage flies rejoice by choice.
The wind forgets to hold its breath,
As dandelions plot their stealthy death.

The sun peeks out from cottony clouds,
While nature laughs and speaks in crowds.
With every rustle, chuckles bloom,
In this grand tale within the room.

So let us join this merry dance,
In nature's whims, we'll take a chance.
For laughter's found in every blade,
In secrets shared beneath the shade.

## Guardian of the Meadow's Decree

A squirrel wears a tiny hat,
He guards the corn, the cheeky brat.
With watchful eyes and fluffy tail,
He chases off the gopher's trail.

Beneath the tree, a wise old crow,
Recites the gossip from below.
With "caws" and laughs, he tells the tale,
Of how the horse lost in the gale.

The flowers giggle in the breeze,
While bees debate who's best with these.
Their buzzing bursts of joyous plots,
Create a buzz that hits the spots.

At twilight's door, they gather 'round,
With wings and wingspan, none a bound.
In silly oaths of grass and clay,
They crown the night with songs of play.

## Enigma of the Silken Turf

A lizard drops his shades and grins,
While pondering over colorful sins.
With every wiggle, every laugh,
He sculpts his way through nature's half.

The flowers wink with petals bright,
As bees dispense their buzzing might.
A butterfly, in haste, slips by,
Chasing a dream that makes it fly.

Oh, chirpy cricket, take your stand,
Delight the world with your command.
In evening's mist, the fun unfolds,
With tales of rapture yet untold.

Beneath the moon, amid soft hops,
The grassy realm just never stops.
A riddle spun, with laughter rife,
In nature's heart, we find our life.

## Anthem of the Forgotten Prairie

A tumbleweed rolls with a grin,
In search of fun where none had been.
Each puff of air gives giggles true,
As it plops down; who knew it too?

The cacti boast with prickled pride,
"Ain't no one who can take this ride!"
And roadrunners dash with frantic feet,
In races that turn delightful heat.

The sunflowers sway, a disco crew,
Spinning to rhythms only they knew.
With silly faces, they strike a pose,
While crickets chirp in comical prose.

So join the fray in golden fields,
Where laughter's harvest never yields.
In each small jest, let spirits soar,
In nature's play, we all explore.

## Murmurs in the Olive Grove

In the grove where olives grow,
Whispers laugh, a jovial show.
Branches dance with a playful sway,
While squirrels plot their nutty play.

The wind giggles through each leaf,
Tickling tales of woe and grief.
Yet every twist and turn we take,
Turns out to be a funny mistake.

A fox prances, a raccoon struts,
Chasing shadows, stepping in ruts.
Each rustle holds a cheeky jest,
In this grove, we laugh the best.

So join the fun, let worries cease,
In olive shade, find sweet release.
For life's too short to fret or moan,
Here, laughter plants its happy throne.

## Parallel Paths of Light and Shadow

Two paths diverge in sunlit glows,
One leads to weeds, the other to prose.
As shadows stretch, the light grew bold,
A race of laughter, a tale retold.

The first path sings a silly tune,
While the second winks at the noon.
Each step a giggle, each hop a cheer,
Light and shadow holding beers.

So if you stumble, don't take fright,
Just blame it on the dance of light.
For every tumble, a chuckle's near,
And shadows whisper what you fear!

In the end, we're all just fools,
Playing games and breaking rules.
In light and dark, we find our way,
With every misstep, we laugh and sway.

## Secrets Between the Stems

Among the stems, there's giggling green,
Flirting wildly, sights unseen.
The daisies whisper jokes and puns,
While ants march on, thinking they've won.

Beneath the leaves, some secrets bloom,
An acorn lies, dreaming of doom.
"Will I grow tall?" it shouts in fright,
"Or will I be a snack tonight?"

The herbs gossip, sharing their sass,
Offering advice like perky grass.
"Just stretch and reach, embrace the sun,
And maybe then you'll be the one!"

So next time you roam among the greens,
Listen for jokes hiding in scenes.
In every stem, a story lies,
Wrapped in giggles and nature's sighs.

## The Poetry of the Hidden Seed

The seed sleeps snug beneath the dirt,
Dreaming of rain and sunny shirt.
"I'll be a tree!" it boasts with pride,
While worms roll eyes, and snicker wide.

This little seed has grand designs,
Imagining branches, grapes, and vines.
Yet here it stays, so tightly bound,
Can't even see the sky around!

When at last the rain pours down,
It shouts, "I'm sprouting!" with a frown.
But up it goes, against all odds,
Becoming more than just a clod.

A twist and turn, and soon it's free,
Laughter ricochets from vine to tree.
For every seed has dreams to sow,
And all of life is just a show!

# The Unseen Chronicles of Green

In the garden, secrets grow,
Each leaf whispers tales, you know.
A worm holds court, with crown of dirt,
While ants parade, all in their shirt.

A squirrel's debate with a butterfly,
Who can leap higher, oh my, oh my!
The daisies giggle, they can't help but sway,
As sunbeams dance, brightening the day.

The rainchecks come, just in the nick,
They play hide and seek, oh what a trick!
With puddles as mirrors, they laugh and splatter,
In the muddy ballet, dreams do scatter.

So here we sit, with laughter in tow,
In this realm where the wild things grow.
Nature's jesters, oh what a scene,
In the chronicles of everything green.

## Reflections from the Gentle Meadow

In the meadow where daisies tumble,
A dandelion tried to be humble.
But with a puff, it lost its cool,
And spread its seeds like a fluffy fool.

The grass takes bets on a ladybug's flight,
Will it spin left, or go right?
With a compass of instinct, it zigzags around,
While crickets chant with a rhythmic sound.

A butterfly flaunts its polka dot dress,
While a bumblebee buzzes without finesse.
Each bloom shines brightly with silly delight,
As the stars come out, twinkling at night.

So join this party, leave worries behind,
In the gentle meadow, where joy's not confined.
With laughter and giggles, the hours conspire,
In a land of enchantment, where fun won't tire.

## Messages from the National Canopy

Up high in the branches, where the squirrels prance,
A woodpecker knocks, join the dance.
The old oak chuckles, its wisdom immense,
As pine needles whisper with green-hued suspense.

The leaves gossip, oh what a sight,
Who wore the best shade between day and night?
A raccoon debates, with its mask so spry,
"Do I look cool? Or just a bit shy?"

The clouds play tag in their fluffy parade,
While shadows stretch long, like an awkward charade.
Each rustle and jolt, a tale to untwist,
In the national canopy, a comic tryst.

So here's to the branches that tickle the sky,
With laughter all around, let worries fly by.
In this shelter of jest, we gather and roam,
Where the canopy laughs, we always feel home.

# Rhapsody of the Sunlit Fields

In the fields where the sunshine spills,
A rabbit hops, overjoyed with thrills.
The sunflowers nod, their tops in a spin,
While the wind joins in, with a breezy grin.

A scarecrow mumbles, 'Where did I go wrong?'
As the crows laugh back, 'You're just too strong!'
Each blade of grass shakes its head with flair,
As daisies shout, 'No worries, don't despair!'

The butterflies twirl in a colorful prank,
While caterpillars mutter, 'We'll join the rank.'
With giggles and wiggles, they frolic all day,
In this sunny rhapsody, come join the fray!

So let's celebrate with each flutter and bound,
In these fields of joy, laughter abounds.
With nature's melody, we dance and we sing,
In the sunlit fields, happiness takes wing.

## Chronicles of the Whispering Leaves

Once a leaf tried to dance in the breeze,
Twisting and turning, as light as you please.
A squirrel stopped short, with eyes open wide,
"What is this madness?" he cried with pride.

The grass whispered secrets to the old oak,
"Tell us your stories, we beg, do not choke!"
The oak said, "Listen, I'm wise, though I'm tall,
But first, give me acorns—then I'll tell all!"

A worm wiggled through with a grand twist of fate,
"I write best from below, don't call me late!"
But flies in a flurry, had stopped in their tracks,
"Worms don't write poems; they're just good at snacks!"

In this comic jangle, all nature's a show,
Where every green blade has tales that they know.
If only the daisies could muster a tune,
We'd boogie all night under the cheeky moon.

## Songs from the Verdant Depths

In the quiet of dusk, a frog croaked a beat,
His friends added chirps, not missing a beat.
A rabbit hopped in, saying, "What's the fuss?"
"Just making a symphony, don't cause a fuss!"

The flowers had petals that were bright and loud,
They sang of warm sunshine to gather a crowd.
A bee buzzing high, joined in with a hum,
"I've got the real buzz, come dance to my drum!"

Then a sleepy old turtle said, "Hold on, wait!"
"Is this how you party? I'll join, it's quite late!"
But to his dismay, as he stretched to boogie,
He tripped on a root—now that's really groovy!

So if you find greenery, lean low and peer,
You might catch a chorus, with laughter and cheer.
Just watch out for ants who may take to the stage,
Their tap-dancing feet are all the rage!

## **Memoirs of the Rustling Blades**

In a field of mischief, the blades held a chat,
One said, "I saw a rabbit steal my hat!"
They giggled with glee, rustling side to side,
"Oh, what a thief, let's go, let's decide!"

A lone dandelion blew, full of hot air,
"I've spread my seeds, let's all share the flair!"
A butterfly flitted, declaring, "I'm grand!"
"But do you have nectar? That's quite how we stand!"

Together they plotted a festival feast,
With ants bringing cookies, a grasshopper beast.
They'd dance in the moonlight, till dawn's early glow,
With tales of the night, and mischief to show.

And so in the meadow, where laughter is found,
The blades weave a story where joy knows no bound.
They champion the fun in the warm summer breeze,
With tips of their leaves, all swaying with ease!

## The Voice of the Prowling Breeze

A sneaky breeze shrieked, "I'm here to invade!"
It tickled the flowers, a truly wild charade.
"Organize a party, I'll help with the sound!"
The petals were ruffled, all danced around!

The tree branches wobbled, saying, "Oh dear!"
"This dancing for wind is far too severe!"
But the breeze just chortled, "You know I'm the best!"
"Let me ruffle your leaves, and put you to the test!"

A rabbit jumped high, in a twisty rabbit jig,
"Hold up, you mere breeze, I'm truly the gig!"
Then the breeze gave a blow with a mighty good laugh,
"Poor bunny, you're cute, but I've got the craft!"

And so in the meadows where the fun never ends,
Breezes toss stories like the best of friends.
If you hear the whispers and giggles so bright,
You might catch a glimpse of this wild wind's flight.

## Nature's Quiet Lament

The trees whisper secrets, so loud yet so shy,
While the squirrels debate who's the funniest guy.
A chipmunk once claimed he could jump to the moon,
Fell short, grabbed an acorn, and hummed a sad tune.

The flowers are chatting with all of their might,
Gossiping 'bout bugs in the soft morning light.
A daisy cracked jokes, made the tulips all grin,
But the roses just blushed, claiming it was a sin.

## Echoes of the Earthbound

The crickets are DJs on a nightly spree,
Dropping the beats for the ants' jubilee.
While cockroaches boogie down low by the wall,
The beetles breakdance, they're having a ball!

The worms in the soil sing a bassline in tune,
With melodies drifted from the light of the moon.
They wriggle and squirm, in a wormy delight,
Joining the chorus, they jam through the night.

## Ode to the Swaying Serenade

The tall grasses sway like they're in a parade,
While the daisies stand guard, all dressed up and displayed.
A breeze brings a tickle, they giggle and shake,
Creating a symphony of laughter and quake.

The butterflies prance in a tutu of wings,
Holding their breath for the sweet songs that sing.
With each flit and flurry, their giggles take flight,
Leaving behind trails of color and light.

## Beneath the Canopy of Dreams

Beneath leafy arches, the critters convene,
Making up stories and plotting their schemes.
A raccoon stole snacks from a picnic delight,
While squirrels played tricks in the soft fading light.

The owls are the judges with wise, warming eyes,
As the hedgehogs compete for the best silly prize.
With laughter and joy, the night stretches on,
Beneath the vast sky where the stars carry on.

## Serenade of the Hidden Roots

In the garden, roots conspire,
Whispering tales of their green attire.
They giggle low, like schoolyard friends,
Waving arms where the soil bends.

A worm plays harp, a beetle beats,
Hosting concerts on the grass so sweet.
The daisies dance, the daisies twirl,
To the rhythm of their earthy whirl.

But watch your step, oh, careful now,
Their secret shows make the daisies bow!
With laughter seeds, they sprout and play,
Under the sun's bright golden ray.

So if you hear that bubbling cheer,
Join the roots for some rooty beer!
For in this patch of verdant delight,
The fun of the garden feels just right.

## Echoes of the Waving Green

The grass sings songs of playful breeze,
Tickling feet like a bunch of tease.
Leaves swirl around on a merry whim,
In a fashion so joyous, it's quite the hymn!

Squirrels join in with their frantic leaps,
While the daisies rock to the chorus heaps.
Frogs croak rhythm, a croaky bass,
As ripples spread through the sunny space.

But when the rains begin to pour,
The grassy giggles turn into roars.
The puddles splash with each bold jump,
The giggling greens all feel a thump!

"Quick, find shelter!" a rabbit cries,
But everyone's busy laughing 'neath the skies.
So when you wander through this scene,
Remember the echoes of the waving green.

## **Legacy of the Soft Fields**

In fields of soft where the daisies bloom,
The skies wear hats, dispelling gloom.
Each butterfly shares a flaky tale,
Of breezy adventures on the wind's sail.

The poppies wink in the honeyed glow,
While lazy bumblebees gather and go.
With laughter stretched across the blue,
They strong-arm the day to feel anew.

But oh, the secrets these fields hold dear,
Like the old tortoise, who's sipping beer!
He tells of time, of laughter-stains,
And how artichokes dance in autumn rains.

So tip your hat to the fields so soft,
And cherish the quirks aloft, aloft!
For in every blade, a joke remains,
In the legacy that laughter gains.

## Chronicle of the Dancing Fern

Ferns flutter whimsically in the glade,
Their dances a secret-their thoughts displayed.
With every sway, they share a jest,
A pun beneath the forest's crest.

Their laughter twirls on a zephyr's song,
While toadstools groove all night long.
"Join us, come, let's laugh and spin!"
The ferns declare with a cheery grin!

A lost sock waltzes, mistaken for fame,
In this forest of whimsy, all play the game.
"Who needs a shoe?" a wise old mouse,
"When dancing at night in the ferny house!"

At dusk, the laughter shimmers bright,
In the glow of the dimming light.
So heed the ferns, oh take your turn,
In the chronicles of the dancing fern.

## Tales of the Verdant Soul

In the meadow, the grass is high,
The ants throw a dance, oh my, oh my!
A snail with a shell, oh what a sight,
Moves like a truck, but just at night.

A frog in a tux, looking quite grand,
Offers fashion tips—who would have planned?
The daisies all giggle, the tulips all sway,
While a gopher spins tales of the grand buffet.

A worm with a dream of a life on the stage,
Imagines a world where he's free from the cage.
He curls up and shimmies, the crowd's in a trance,
Cheering for more of his wiggly dance!

So here's to the green, and its quirky charm,
Where laughter grows loud, and no one's alarmed.
In this silly land where the wild things play,
The grass tells its jokes in a whimsical way.

## Chronicles of the Verdant Grove

In the grove where the critters conspire and tease,
A squirrel with a acorn claims to have cheese.
But the cheese turns to mud, splatters the floor,
As the rabbit retorts, 'What a mess, it's a chore!'

The shadows grow long, and the hedgehogs unite,
To brainstorm new schemes for a top-notch fright.
They plan for the night, with their spiky attire,
Creating a spook that'll surely inspire!

The trees hold their breath, and the crickets obey,
While a turtle runs laps in a pretty fast way.
"Who knew I could zoom?" he exclaims with a grin,
Just to trip on a root—oh where to begin?

So gather 'round friends, for this tale's just begun,
In a world where mishaps are always such fun.
With laughter and joy, the creatures convene,
Creating a tale that's a sight to be seen.

# Secrets in the Soft Green

Beneath blades of emerald, whispers arise,
Of secrets held tight, and excellent pies.
The ladybugs gossip, the beetles all nod,
'Bout the fox who dreams of being a god.

A hedgehog once claimed he could fly with a cheer,
But confusion ensued when the crows drew near.
With wings made of wishes, he soared through the sky,
Only to find that he's quite good at shy!

The daisies all snicker, the lilies all laugh,
As the spider retorts, "Let's take a nice bath!"
In the puddles they giggle, with bubbles of glee,
While a toad croaks a tune of pure harmony.

So listen, dear friend, to this land of delight,
Where shenanigans happen from morning till night.
The secrets reside in the soft gentle green,
In a world full of laughter, it's the best you've seen.

## Harmonies of the Leafy Realm

In the leafy domain, the music's sublime,
A caterpillar waltzes, takes things one rhyme.
The woodpecker drums on a hollowed-out tree,
While the sloths hold a party—so slow, can't you see?

The mushrooms all jiggle, the ferns hum a tune,
In a chorus of giggles beneath the bright moon.
As the crickets recite poetry so fine,
While the snails play their trumpets, a sound so divine.

The bumblebees buzz with a rhythm so sweet,
Chatting about honey and new dance steps to greet.
The butterflies flutter, performing a show,
In a ballet of color that steals the whole show!

So join in the fun, and feel the delight,
In this leafy realm, where the oddball takes flight.
With laughter and music, let's take to the skies,
In this happy green world, where joy never dies.

## Verses from the Grassland Mystics

In fields where whispers dance and play,
A cow once tried to join a ballet.
She leapt and twirled, quite full of glee,
Then tripped and landed, oh dear me!

The sheep convened, in cloaks of wool,
To gossip 'neath the tree so cool.
They spoke of dreams of endless grass,
And who could leap the highest pass.

A sneaky hare with tricks to spare,
Brought laughter to the sunny square.
He painted spots on every toad,
And told them laughter is the road!

So listen close when fields do call,
For nature's jokes will cover all.
With grass beneath and sky so wide,
Each giggle grows with joy and pride.

## Pilgrimage of the Nature's Call

A turtle set out, with dreams so grand,
To find the best buffet in the land.
He asked the breeze for some advice,
"Where can I find those greens so nice?"

The crow cawed out, with feathery sass,
"Turtle, just watch out for that fast grass!"
The turtle sighed, with a wink and nod,
"Now that would be a greenish fraud!"

With petals in hand, the flowers danced,
Each petal draped as fate entranced.
A bee buzzed close, making his case,
"I'll mingle with flowers, but keep my place!"

And so they roamed, this mismatched crew,
In search of greens, and skies of blue.
With laughter echoing, they'd all agree,
Nature's pilgrimage is wild and free.

## The Quiet Rumble of Nature's Voice

A squirrel was stashing nuts with flair,
But forgot where he put them, unaware.
His friends all laughed, hiding their glee,
As he searched each branch of the old oak tree.

The wind whispered tales, quite absurd,
Of frogs that dreamed of being unheard.
They croaked their songs, thinking they sung,
In harmony, like bells that rung!

A worm in the soil, thinking it's profound,
Claimed he knew all that spun 'round.
"Just listen, dear friends, to my earthy spree,
I hold secrets deep, under this leafy spree!"

But laughter erupted from high above,
As branches swayed in the gentle shove.
With nature's giggles, it was clear to see,
A joyful ruckus in every spree.

## The Untold Stories of the Soil

In the soil, secrets creep,
Worms tell tales, while roots keep.
Fungi giggle, sharing lore,
Underneath, they dance and snore.

Moles plot mischief, sprout some glee,
While ladybugs sip their tea.
Dandelions blow, with a puff,
Saying, 'Life's too short, be tough!'

Caterpillars join the fun,
Chomping leaves, not on the run.
They flip and wriggle, what a sight,
Saying, 'Larva party, day or night!'

So dig a hole, join the cheer,
Listen close, the soil's near.
Nature's gossip, bright and spry,
Whispers softly, 'Just give a try!'

## **Breath of the Verdant Spirits**

Leaves are whispering, giggling high,
As breezes come and flutter by.
The ferns convene with tales to weave,
While willow winks, 'Just believe!'

Clouds stumble as they drift along,
Tripping over their own song.
A squirrel chuckles at their fall,
'Oh dear sky, do you need a call?'

The daisies burst in laughter bright,
Telling jokes that take to flight.
Sunbeams shine with glee all day,
While shadows murmur, 'Hooray, hooray!'

Each gust of wind shares a charm,
With every rustle, life's a farm.
Join the fun, leave gloom behind,
In this green world, joy you'll find!

## **Tides of the Emerald Sea**

In the grass, waves rise and fall,
Blades sway, laugh, and call.
Dancing like a crew of sprites,
Underneath the sun's warm lights.

A snail sings in a conch shell,
While ants march on, oh so swell.
Crickets chirp a lively tune,
Singing praises to the moon.

Jumping bugs, they leap and prance,
While bees buzz in a happy dance.
Tall blades poke their neighbors' sides,
'Watch out! Here come the grassblade rides!'

With every wind, a new decree,
Nature spreads its humor free.
So take a seat, enjoy the spree,
In this emerald jubilee!

## The Blessing of the Sunlit Blades

Oh, sunlit blades, bright and spry,
Tickle toes as you wave by.
Your laughter floats on summer's breath,
In fields where joy defies all death.

Blades of green, with pranks to play,
Invite each critter out to play.
Grasshoppers host a bouncing show,
Where giggles leap and laughter flows.

The sun peeks down with a wink,
While shadows below start to think.
'This grass is wild, a playful land,
Where every dance is unplanned!'

So join the blades in their bright game,
Nature's prank is never lame.
With every sway, hearts feel the cheer,
Out in the fields, joy draws near!

## In Praise of the Rooted Ones

In the garden, worms play chess,
Their moves are slow, who'd have guessed?
With a wink, the daisies cheer,
While bees hum tunes quite unclear.

Every root holds a secret tale,
Of cracked pots and runaway snails.
They gossip beneath the morning dew,
As ants march by, forming a queue.

With tiny hats, the kids take flight,
On dandelion clouds, pure delight.
Roots giggle when the rain might fall,
"Just another shower, we love it all!"

Let's toast the grass with cups of tea,
And dance with the breeze, wild and free.
Here's to the grounded, who never roam,
Their laughter makes every patch feel like home.

## Nature's Quiet Testament

In silence, rocks tell stories grand,
Of rain and time and shifting sand.
Giggling leaves whisper things so sweet,
While acorns plan their next big feat.

The flowers hold a beauty spree,
Petals trolling bees so carelessly.
Sunshine laughs, tickling roots below,
While clouds debate the best rain to show.

A squirrel hops with a nutty grin,
"Who needs a crown when you're king within?"
Each twig has a jingle, a jig, a tune,
Nature's party under the bright, pale moon.

So here's to the witnesses unseen,
Who watch us shuffle, jive, and preen.
Let's toast to laughter, both big and small,
In the quiet spots, the best fun of all!

## The Untold Stories of the Earth

In cracks of the sidewalk, secrets hide,
Daisies pop through, all dignified.
Old stones chuckle, cracking up wide,
While four-leaf clovers wink, filled with pride.

Each raindrop holds a snippet of mirth,
It tickles the grass, oh what a birth!
Slugs glide by in a slimy race,
While crickets leap, don't skimp on pace!

The trees clap branches in rhythm divine,
Creating a canopy cocktail, so fine!
Mushrooms giggle in colors so bright,
Graduating high from fungi delights.

So let's gather 'round this lively scene,
Where laughter's rich and feels like a dream.
To the silent jesters, let's raise a cheer,
For the untold stories that draw us near!

## Whispers of the Living Soil

Beneath our feet, a chatter starts,
A banquet where the dirt imparts.
Worms share jokes that tickle the roots,
As moles dance in their snazzy boots.

Underneath the leafy canopy,
Fungi laugh in stealthy jubilee.
Wind stirs giggles, whispers on high,
Telling stories only the bugs can pry.

Beetles march to a tapping song,
While carrots brace for their crop, so long!
Nature's comedy, a quirky affair,
Full of jesters from here to there.

So here's to the magic below the ground,
Where laughter and life abound all around.
Let's join the fun, a jubilee shared,
In the soil's embrace, we're wildly spared!

www.ingramcontent.com/pod-product-compliance
Lightning Source LLC
Chambersburg PA
CBHW072145200426
43209CB00051B/575